The Echo of Heartbeats

The Echo of Heartbeats

Alan Gilbert

This is a work of fiction all of the characters, names, incidents, organizations and dialogue in this book are either products of the author's imagination or are used fictitiously.

ISBN #:	978-1-4476-6214-3
Content ID:	10530082
Book Title:	The Echo of Heartbeats

“Like butterflies in spring poetry awakens the spirit, stirs the imagination and explores the possibilities with each stroke of its rhythmic wings”

Jamie Lynn Morris

About the Author

Born in Southampton, England, Alan Gilbert attended the West of England school and St Lloys College Exeter. He took his degree in Psychology and art at The Open University graduating in 1984. Alan and his wife Barbara, have three grown children. He lives in Southampton.

Other poetry books by Alan Gilbert.

All That Rhymes With Love.	March 2010.
Love is a Dreamer.	November 2010.

Preface

Along with the advent and rapid popularity of social networking there has come a resurgence in the arts in general, and poetry in particular. After a long decline in its appeal, once again poetry and poetry groups are thriving. Technology has opened up channels for easy publication, discussion and critique that have been severely restricted before. These groups have rapidly become forums where modern and more tradition styles of the art are at the core of a new upsurge in interest that is willing both to revisit the past and experiment with new forms of the poet's art.

Alan Gilbert 2011.

For the heartbeat.

Contents

A Whispered Dream   Part 1

She whispered, "Come and dance
The orange sun has left the sky,
And all the stars are drifting
They just wait for you and I."

She whispered, "Take my hand
I'll lead you to my secret place,
Where moonlights silver glow
Will etch a smile upon your face."

She whispered, "Hush my love
Come lay beside the crystal stream,
For I will stay with you a while
And leave you such a dream."

She whispered, "Oh my love
The golden sun does touch the sky,
Before its rays caress my face
I must this place forever fly."

She whispered, "Still my love
For I will come again to you,
Once these stars have turned again
And both our worlds are new."

A Whispered Dream Part 2

She whispered, "Wake my love
It's time to leave your mortal sleep,
For all the stars have turned and I
My vow to you will keep."

She whispered, "See my love
The moon has risen blue and white,
And all the magic of its glow
Will shine on us tonight."

She whispered, "Come my love
Tonight we fly on silent wings,
Across the ocean known as time
Where love forever sings."

She whispered. "Now my love
Come and take me by the hand,
So all the mysteries of love
You then will understand."

As Much as I

No Walls could ever hold her
Nor let her spirit fly,
For surely freedom loves her
But not as much as I.

No dullness could suppress her
Nor smile in her eye,
For surely laughter loves her
But not as much as I.

No season could desert her
Nor spring or summer fly,
For surely nature loves her
But not as much as I.

No music could deny her
Nor let her rhythm die,
For surely muses love her
But not as much as I.

Of Freedom

Tell me where did freedom go
I hear you weeping,
Was it stolen stealthy, slow
While we were sleeping.
Did it simply fade away
Taken for granted every day,
As we forgot that sacred way
Was in our keeping?

What of those who went before
In all that sorrow,
To keep the faith they gave no more
Than their tomorrow.
Did we simply shed a tear
Stand in silence once a year,
Then let ourselves be cowed in fear
Our promise hollow?

So how are we to turn the tide
That's overflowing,
When did we learn a nation's pride
Is not for showing,
We can no longer stand aside
Imagining the cause has died,
But make it clear to those who lied
Our angers growing?

A Memory of Rooms

Here in a nursery
No cry was heeded,
Hunger was often
Love never seen.

Look out a window
Where is the child?
Footprints though fading
Show where he has been.

Stand in a hallway
Child bewildered,
Lost in confusion
Stares at a scene.

Lay in a bedroom
Rain on a window,
Tear to be waking
A terrible dream.

Pale in a mirror
Images moving,
Form and reforming
Labels on tombs.

Walk in a shadow
Voice in a whisper,
Destined to carry
A memory of rooms.

Concerto in Red

She looks, the devil
Flashing in her eyes,
Half turns her head
Her smile lingers still.
Then reaching out
Skin lightly touches skin,
That one caress alone
A sensuous thrill.

More red than passion
Woven to a gown,
That swirls and settles
Showing nature's art.
Now loose and falling
Softly on the floor
In scarlet overture
To beauties part.

Now the wayward
Moonlight in the room,
Projects two shadows
Mingled on the wall.
That move in time
To that eternal theme,
Of nature's dance
To love's primeval call.

How Wonderful the Night

How wonderful the night
When long felt passions meet,
The touch of silk on silk
Caressing hands and feet.

The thrill of clouded eyes
Anticipation of each touch,
Shared sensual ecstasy
Was never felt so much.

How will the pleasure fall?
From hands or lips or ice,
How pleasing to the heart
To practice such a vice.

I Wonder

I wonder can you tell me
Why are flat fish flat,
And how did such a creature
Get to be like that.
It can't be easy tying up
A bright cravat,
Or even wearing glasses
And a broad brimmed hat.

I wonder can you tell me
Does a dog fish bark,
And can you take it walkies
In the down town park.
Would it chase a rabbit
In the Forest for a lark,
Or sniff the trail of someone
It was tracking in the dark.

I wonder can you tell me
Does a sword fish fence,
Swagger like a musketeer
In search of recompense.
Or maybe fight a duel
In a maids defence,
Or does it simply whittle wood
And show more sense.

I wonder can you tell me
Does a cat fish purr,
Go around in whiskers
And a coat of tabby fur.
If you took it to a cat show
Would it cause a stir,
For the judges couldn't say
If it was a him or her.

Letter from Passchendaele

Mary gal there's summit I must say
Today we as this briefin from the searge,
He says all leave is cancelled right away
An those as disobeys is on a charge.

He then goes on to say we as a week
To write a letter ome to those we love,
And put our ouse in order so to speak
We's moving up to join the final shuv.

Gal you knows the way it is with me
Whose never held a gun or owned a knife,
An now I'm finkin ows it gunna be
To hold your aim an take another's life.

Now I as erd some tales from those sent back
Shattered, mad, or blinded every one,
Who sez the generals ought to get the sack
They'll kill us bloody all before they're done.

I only writes this letter in me head
Cos these are things I really wanna say,
To you I write heroic things instead
We're off to glory and a brighter day.

The Faerie Dance

Now the coppice still as evening
Cloaked in shadow's sombre weaves,
Slowly wakes as autumn breezes
Stir the slumber of the leaves.

As the midnight hour approaches
Now the harvest moon is high,
Comes the strain of faerie music
Softer than a wood nymph's sigh.

There at the appointed moment
Gold and silver wings appear,
Thus the faerie dancers promise
The fertile earth another year.

Sometimes at the Dead of Night

Sometimes at dead of night she calls
Echoing down corridors of dreams,
Lost at crossroad in another land
Tumbling in confusion.

Her plaintive cry sinks into my soul
Heartbreaking sorrow and despair,
Swirling all the colours of her mind
Into forgotten rainbows.

Her captive spirit aches to be set free
Its melancholy tears are pools of doubt,
Enchanted by a spell cast long ago
On some far horizon.

Tell me in Springtime

Tell me in springtime
When new life is growing,
Whisper the secret
Of love that keeps flowing.
Speak to me softly
Young birds are sleeping,
Show me the signs
Of a new season creeping.

Tell me in the summer
On those walks by the ocean,
Our halcyon days
Spent in quite devotion.
Paint me that picture
The one from your dreams,
Of horses in meadows
By the clear crystal streams.

Tell me in autumn
That season you love,
Leaves flaming colour
Drift down from above.
A host of red berries
Sharp chill in the air,
Such peace for the soul
Just to be with you there.

Tell me in winter
While snowflakes are falling,
We'll run through the fields
When the pale sun is falling.
As we laze by the fire
While music is playing,
We'll dream about spring
And the old year decaying.

Me and You and Kerrie Ann

We sailed out on that summer's day
Just me you and Kerrie Ann,
Out to the islands in the bay
To where we knew the dolphins ran.

And as the wind blew from the west
For me and you and Kerrie Ann,
It gave each wave a silver crest
And billowed sails with nature's fan.

We stopped and anchored out at sea
Did me and you and Kerrie Ann,
The day was peaceful as could be
Most tranquil backdrop for our plan.

But as we watched the dolphins play
For me and you and Kerrie Ann,
We never saw the sky turn grey
Or noticed how those currents ran.

You never made the slightest sound
Just slipped from me and Kerrie Ann,
And now you never will be found
Out in the bay where dolphins ran.

Now every summer's day I sit
Down by the quay with Kerrie Ann,
Though all her timbers rot and pit
And all her sails are torn and wan.

Touch

Deep black heaven
A sprinkling of stars,
Twinkling silver specks
Of Infinite wonder.

On such a night
The galaxy unfolds,
To grace the soul
Exquisitely sublime.

Now hopelessly lost
Rejoicing in splendour,
Falling through time
You touch my hand.

The Promise

Awake you sleeping spirits
You knights from days of old,
You guardians of Britain
In myth and legend told.
Arise and keep the promise
A vow you made that when,
Your country needed heroes
We'd hear you ride again.

You denizens of Camelot
Who took that sacred vow,
The table and Excalibur
Are waiting for you now.
Again to swear allegiance
And songs of valour sing,
For Britain and for Arthur
Our once and future king.

Awake you loyal bowmen
You men in Lincoln green,
Take up your song of freedom
That made old Sherwood ring.
The time for slumbers over
You merry men who stood,
For England and for freedom
With Robin of the hood.

Snowflakes

Flakes of snow as blossom off the trees
Swirl and dance all wafted by a breeze,
Pure perfection height of nature's art
Though formed from ice themselves,
Would warm the coldest heart.

I cannot watch so turn my head away
For all that beauty will not let me stay,
And if I bide I know that tears will start
Those snowflakes dance as one,
We lovers waltz apart.

And yet I have no reason to complain
For I was lost, would never love again,
A life of grey deprived of brighter hue
Then drifting like a wondrous flake,
Came beauty that is you.

The Favour

Tonight the hell of battle calls
Knights are gathered in the halls,
Border guards have come to say
The tyrant's armies crossed today.

Peasants with their cows and sheep
Are gathered in the castle keep,
When his marauders cross the land
They burn and kill on either hand.

My lady I must take my leave
Don my breastplate and my greave,
My fellow knights do wait below
And we must ride to face this foe.

One boon I would beg of you
That I may wear your ribbons blue,
Thus all the other knights may see
That of them all you favour me.

And when the battle's at its height
Though danger rides to left and right,
I'll know through all I fight for thee
That you may live unharmed and free.

My lady your true knight will be
This hour a man of chivalry,
So neither friend nor foe can say
I failed to honour you this day.

Hush Hush

Hush, hush my eager heart
This night is falling fast,
With blue enchanted hours
For loves impassioned part.

Cool, cool my heated blood
That warms me into fire,
This race is still to run
With this vision of desire.

Slow, slow my streaming mind
Constant images unwind,
Visions in abstraction
Love and fantasy entwined.

Stay, stay impatient time
Why always keen to go?
Does nothing ever seem to you
Much sweeter taken slow.

Pagan Christmas

This time, the darkest of the year
We will gather, everyone,
Asking with humility
To send us back the sun.
Grant to us a fertile earth
Wherein our crops will grow,
And pray the land will live again
After the frost and snow.

We bring to decorate the hall
The Holly and the ivy green,
Sprigs of sacred mistletoe
Its berries white and clean.
We offer up these humble gifts
Though unworthy everyone,
And prey our Mother smiles upon
Her children every one.

The Silence was Bliss

Tami and Jason were born to be lovers
Met in the park in games with the others,
When he first saw her smile
Their story began
That night in his bedroom
The images ran.
All heat and confusion
No sense to all this.
His thoughts were exciting
The silence was bliss.

As Tami saw him her heart started falling
Romantic by nature her future was calling,
As she wrote in her diary
Alone in her room,
She drew at the bottom
A bride with a groom.
Then she drifted to sleep
Still thinking of this.
Her dreams were of loving
The silence was bliss.

Love is a flower that grows in the sun
One Friday in May the two became one,
They spent time by the ocean
Their first time away,
To the rhythm of breakers
Two bodies at play.
When sleep came upon them
They dreamed about this.
As night closed around them
The silence was bliss.

Now in the rooms they rented from others
Furniture given by fathers and mothers,
The world closes upon them
Soon making demand's
There is industry round them
But none wanting hands.
Stung by every refusal
He would rage about this.
When he slept from the drinking
The silence was bliss.

Daily his anger would reach a new height
Looking for reasons to argue or fight,
When he lashed out and hit her
She was scared for her life,
With his hands at her throat
She struck with a knife.
Though she'd acted from terror
Had never meant this.
There was blood on her hands
But the silence was bliss.

Roses

Tell me where will roses grow?
Why, in the garden as you know,
But there the sun can burn them so
As they are cooled by winter snow.

Tell me will they flourish there?
They are at ease in nature's care,
And will their perfume fill the air
The breeze will waft it everywhere.

Tell me will they stay so small?
No, sun and rain will make them tall,
So will their blood red petals fall?
In time they must surrender all.

Tell me what they signify?
They stand for love that will not die,
Then why is it that lovers cry?
The thorns can cut you by and by.

Thoughts from a London Night

Walk any city rain soaked street
Vile rotting garbage round your feet,
Grim shadows hide a thousand fears
Slum tenements with blood and tears.

Banshee sirens wake the night
Rape, murder, riot, dealers fight,
For each the wailing sounds the same
Hear God and devil play their game.

Ride crowded subways, see the eyes
Reflecting hatred, fear, and lies,
So many lonely faces stare
Aspects haggard with despair.

Work in your pretty halls of glass
Walk where laden shoppers pass,
Meet in cafes with your own,
Phantoms wait for you at home.

Will

Will I ever walk beside her
Laughing in evening air,
Will I turn my head from reading
Glad to find her sitting there.
Will she dream upon my pillow
Far away from worldly care,
Shall I love her as the sunrise
Lights the colours in her hair?

Will she ever find me waiting
Just because the day was long,
And I found with every hour
Emptiness while she was gone.
Is there waiting in our future
Everything we two have planned,
Just to dwell at peace with nature
With the creatures and the land?

Will we know the joy of loving
When two hearts are so in tune,
And the sound of our concerto
Echoes through the afternoon.
Will we sit and talk till sunrise
Wishing on each shooting star,
Always new things to be learning
Others staying as they are?

The First Frost

Last night the frost came
Stealthily creeping,
Touching the land
With its icy caress.
Walked through the city
Naked and freezing
Clothing the trees
In a wintery dress.

Last night the frost came
Breathing on window's
Clouding the view
With a silvery sheen.
Crept down the dark allies
Long before morning,
Leaving the garbage
To sparkle and gleam.

Last night the frost came
Swiftly and silent,
Painting the world
With a misting of White.
The bright moon revealing
A picture of winter,
Nature's transition
A beautiful sight.

Tell me the Night

Tell me night
Is dark for you as well,
Sometimes awake
You crave the morning bell.
Tell me your heart
Is aching just the same,
And that the missing's
Not a childish game.

Tell me the silence
Sometimes makes you cry,
Longing to hear
That call as hours fly.
Wondering if
Somehow the feeling died,
Longing to see you
From the other's side.

Tell the loving
Sometimes make you weak,
Scatters your thoughts
Each time you try to speak.
Tumbling, falling
Into love's embrace,
Praying to live
Forever in this grace.

Tell me our song
Is such a fine duet,
Sung to a tune
Our hearts will not forget.
Formed from the words
Apollo bade us rhyme,
They speak of our love
And echo for all time.

The Death of Blixton

Do you see along the headlands
Where the cliff has crumbled down,
Once a host of people lived there
In a thriving market town.
Just some ordinary people
Each the same as you and me,
Yet they all were killed at midnight
In October sixty- three.

Records say the day was placid
Autumn sunshine filled the sky,
Children played along the headlands
Chasing carts that trundled by.
The Market place was all a bustle
Flags and bunting everywhere,
The schoolgirls choir was at practice
Wild flowers in their hair.

All the weeks of work were over
Founders day was dawning soon,
Every street rang out with laughter
Well into that afternoon.
All the people were elated
Never stopped to question why,
The sun was lost, completely hidden
By the blackness of the sky.

By six o-clock the rain was falling
Sheets of lightning lit the sky,
Winds were tearing at the shutters
Howling like a banshee cry.
Seas were raging like a tempest
Waves like mountains hit the shore,
By ten o-clock the folk were frightened
Never seen the like before.

At the cliffs the waves were crashing
Each one like a hammer blow.
Sending chunks of solid rock face
Falling to the sea below.
Out at sea a vessel floundered
Thrown like driftwood to the shore,
Men while fighting for existence
Prayers for mercy did implore.

The captain was a man of iron
Death had stalked him many times,
Now he knew he'd lose the battle
So terrible the ship inclines.
Then a roar that drowned the thunder
Shock waves brought him to his knee,
As he watched transfixed in horror
Blossom town fell into the sea.
Bottom of Form

Arrival

How the days and nights had lingered
Slow the waiting time declines,
Calendar was stained and fingered
Being checked so many times.
Now at last the day was dawning
Now the waiting time had passed,
While his bleary world was yawning
She was coming home at last.

Driving up was all frustration
Queues and gridlocks everywhere,
When he reached his destination
There were minutes left to spare.
Just some minutes left to find her
In this people crowded place,
Suddenly he stood behind her
Then she turned to his embrace.

Brown Eyes Trilogy 1

Brown eyes won't you tell me
What is it that you seek,
What is that echo in your voice
I hear each time we speak.
Why is your gaze so wistful
When looking at your star,
Are you hoping for the answers
To find out who you are.

Brown eyes have you wondered
When rainbows light the sky,
Why if you try to chase them
Their colours fade and die.
Or, on waking in the morning
A dream still in your head,
Although you try to hold it
It slips away instead.

Brown eyes have you pondered
When hearing breakers roar,
The miles they have travelled
To reach this distant shore.
Like you upon your journey
To who you want to be,
May lose your point of reference
Like those waves upon the sea.

Brown eyes life's a journey
We started long ago,
Exactly where its leading
Not one of us can know.
So each day as you travel
Remember as you do,
It's the journey that's the joy of life
Not where its leading to.

Brown Eyes Trilogy 2

Brown eyes I remember
That look upon your face,
All the world to choose from
For you there was no place.
All those stars you wished on
Would never tell you how,
To find the path you needed
The one you're walking now.

Brown eyes deep inside you
Was who you sought to be,
Not whispered on a glimmer
From a far flung galaxy.
It was there to be discovered
It was burning in your soul,
It was waiting for that moment
To live and make you whole.

Brown eyes now I see you
And I almost want to cry,
For joy can overwhelm me
When I watch your spirit fly.
Brown eyes you may stumble
As you travel on your way,
But a spirit burns inside you
That will never fade away.

Brown Eyes Trilogy 3

Brown eyes do you remember
I spoke with you that day,
I found you gazing at your star
So many miles away.
We talked of roaring breakers
And drifting on the sea,
I never got to say that you
Are beautiful to me.

You looked so very wistful
And seemed so far away,
Eyes had never shone so bright
As brown eyes did that day.
You said your soul was drifting
Not knowing where to go,
You had so much to tell a world
That didn't want to know.

I told you life's a journey
That leads to who knows where,
You told me there are reasons
For all the things we share.
I wanted so to show you
The things you couldn't see,
Now looking back I understand
That you were teaching me.

Brown eyes come sit beside me
Let me take you by the hand,
You know how sometimes feelings
Overwhelm the things we planned.
We've travelled far together
And both have changed it's true,
You've come to mean so much to me
Dear brown eyes I love you.

We who Dream

Come gaze into the water love
Down through the turquoise of the sea,
To where the queen of mermaids lives
Who writes the scripts for you and me.
Her pages are the purest gold
Her pens are rainbow fishes hair,
And there she writes the fairy tales
For lover's hearts and dreams to share.

We'll go deep in the forest glade
Just at the rising of the moon,
And hear the king of unicorns
Composing every lover's tune.
His harp is darkest ebony
The strings, vine's of ancient tree,
He writes the songs the river sings
And serenades for you and me.

As bronze and amber fleck the sky,
And watch a rainbow being made
To paint a shower by and by.
The queen and all her fairy maids
Mix fruits with secret magic dyes,
Then let it go to catch the sun
And be reflected in your eyes.

Chasing Something

Those were the days
Do you recall,
When we were young
And dads were tall.
The sunny days
Would come and go,
Now looking back
I miss them so.

The years they flew
So fast it seems,
We stretched our arms
To catch our dreams.
Now here I stand
And wonder why,
I chased a dream
That made me cry.

Yet still I know
That such is fate,
Don't end the show
It's not too late.
There still is time
For one more dream,
An open door
A loving theme.

I Imagine Winter Evenings

I imagine winter evenings
We two sitting by the fire,
North wind cooling everything
But never our desire.
I remember glancing at you
In the dancing fires glow,
And wondering what I had done
That you should love me so.

In the short time that I've known you
You have always been the same,
Forever laughing in the sunshine
And dancing in the rain.
I will never cease to wonder
How in you is reconciled,
All the passions of a woman
With the magic of a child.

Seasons

When all the seasons I recall
Winter, summer, spring and fall,
They each show beauty but of all
The spring is most serene.

Summer speaks of lazy ways
Golden fields and holidays,
Fishing where the rainbow plays
And dipping in the stream.

See when autumn turns around
Burnished leaves of gold are found,
Strewn in carpets on the ground
Like petals from a dream.

Winter's cloak is purest white
That falls in silence overnight,
Stars are seen to shine so bright
And cast a silver sheen.

Then the springtime, Queen of all
Buds are shooting, showers fall,
Nature's promise to us all
Of summer lush and green.

Snowflakes

Flakes of snow as blossom off the trees
Swirl and dance all wafted by a breeze,
Pure perfection height of nature's art
Though formed from ice themselves,
Would warm the coldest heart.

I cannot watch so turn my head away
For all that beauty will not let me stay,
And if I bide I know that tears will start
Those snowflakes dance as one,
We lovers waltz apart.

And yet I have no reason to complain
For I was lost, would never love again,
A life of grey deprived of brighter hue
Then drifting like a wondrous flake,
Came beauty that is you.

The Timeless River Flow

See the timeless river flow
Meandering for ever
In the valley there below.

Always moving calm and slow
While nourishing the heather
See the timeless river flow.

Continuing in sun and snow
Reflections of the weather
In the valley there below.

Rippled as the breezes blow
The eddies dance together
See the timeless river flow.

A place where wild flowers grow
Can lose its charm, but never
In the valley there below.

Fallen petals drifting slow
Sailing with a feather,
In the valley there below
See the timeless river flow.

Think of a Time

Think of a time you stumbled in your life
Feeling a way as one with clouded sight,
Falling through empty spaces day to day
Begging some unknown spirit for the light.

Think of a day that dawned to find you lost
Wandering lonely in some crowded street,
Everything won was at too high a cost
Then given away, surrendered in defeat.

Think of the day the darkest one of all
Finding the fight no longer worth the prize,
Peeling your mind like paper from a wall
Abandoning hope to feel redemption rise.

Think of the moment, you alone may know
What lit the flame that kindled deep inside,
A letter, a call, a thought from long ago
An echo of love that turned that awful tide.

Flight of the Gypsy Queen

He was a gypsy a wandering heart
Sleeping in starlight and dancing in rain,
Adrift on the land without compass or chart
Asking to work for his supper in vain.

She was a young queen of title and land
Heir to a palace of marble and gold,
Princes would visit to ask for her hand
Promising fortunes to have and to hold.

As she was walking a balustrade high
Taking the air on some halcyon day,
A voice started singing as soft as a sigh
As the young gipsy came walking her way.

Singing to maids as they hurried on by
Hoping to find a hospitable place,
As he looked up he first caught her eye
Gasped at the beauty he saw in her face.

Now as she saw him just sauntering there
She suddenly realised how she was alone,
Before her a life only burdened with care
The glittering castle a prison not home.

She ran down a stairway where no eye could see
Ridding herself of her cumbersome gown,
Out to the yard where two horses would be
Owned by a prince who had come to the town.

She and her father had often been riding
Her skill in the saddle so seldom is seen,
Once he had said to her, playfully chiding
"You ride a mare more a soldier than queen."

Out from the palace the stallion thundered
Down to a lane where her gypsy was seen,
No word was needed, yet often he wondered
How he with a look won the heart of a queen.

The gypsy was hunted by many a soldier
Many a nobleman searching were seen,
Far in secret glade often he'd hold her
Life was a blessing for gypsy and queen.

Charm

You took my hands
Though they were cold,
Redeemed my body
Young for old.
Returned my silver
Hair to gold
And said it was a dream.

You stole the shadow
From my eyes,
Replaced the dark
With starry skies.
Then softly laughed
At my surprise
And said inhale the theme.

You kissed a smile
From every frown,
Our bodies danced
In Eider down.
We fell so deep
As if to drown
In passions racing stream.

Don't think me Gone

I am not gone
Please never think me so,
The world must turn
Tides ebb, and spirits grow.
Our souls evolve
As everything must do,
Though bodies fade
My essence stays with you.

It's nature's way
That everything must change,
All bodies grow
Then fall to rearrange.
But nothings lost
Just takes a different form,
Our souls remain
Complete as when we're born.

Some summer days
You'll feel me close at hand,
The softest breeze
That whispers in the sand.
A gentle touch
Much lighter than a kiss,
And you may know
That life is more than this.

So talk to me
And wait for my reply,
For every soul
Was given wings to fly.
And I will answer
Everything you say,
I won't forsake you
For a single day.

Abandoned Love

He sings the saddest songs
The world has known,
And wanders miles
In search of solitude.
These days a smile
Would seldom cross his lips,
Just heavy heart
And melancholy mood.

And all that he can do
Is wonder why,
They never talk of
Anything so deep.
Now all their words are
Shallow skimming stones,
And all his nights are
Voids of dreamless sleep.

And still they walk
Together every day,
They laugh with friends
Word perfect in their part.
But all his thoughts
Are of another world,
Abandoned love
Is poison to the heart.

Stella

Stella was the petal from a rose
A leaf of beauty fallen from the bloom,
Who, carried on the wings of broken dreams
Would share her tears and kisses with the moon.

She lived among remains of withered hearts
Her eyes were cursed from watching their decay,
She stole away in clammy, fevered dreams,
To cleanse the vile corruption of the day.

Such visions will infect a troubled soul
No human spirit can itself sustain,
Yet she was christened child of a star
Whose distant orbit was in flux again.

Storm

Alert the watch all hands all hands on deck
Aloft and set the storm sails, make them fast,
Then rig the ratlines tight from stem to stern
The seas are up, we're heading for a blast.

Unfast the boats and toss them to the storm
The dervish wind will crush them into splints,
Then lash the forty cannon to the deck
No man will rest so each surpass their stints.

You surgeon's boys now to your station go
Make keen each edge and mark your master well,
If God has grace to gift to you the dawn
You will no longer fear the wrath of hell.

There is no time to pray no place for fear
No time to ponder on the hours ahead,
Now everyman must make his peace alone
I fear that fate has marked us living dead.

Boudicca Warrior Queen

See over there beside the ancient wood
As the slate escarpment meets the stream,
That is a place where once an army stood
Summoned by the war cry of a Queen.

Britain was a seething fractured land
Many warlords held their own domain,
Roaming at night with murderous intent
And any who resisted would be slain.

This the age when all the world was Rome
Legions came and mighty kingdoms fell,
They offered civil rule to those subdued
Those who yearned for freedom, only hell.

A fragile peace had settled on the land
As one by one the tribes of Britain fell,
But fate has restless hands that never sleep
And how they work their purpose none can tell.

It happened on the feast of Bacchus eve
A raucous night of laughter lust and wine,
In Anglia a dreadful wrong was done
That echoes down the corridors of time.

One rabble of the Roman army there
A drunken time of revelry had seen,
And by some dreadful circumstance unknown
Raped and killed the daughters of the Queen.

When news of this abomination came
There was a screen of unremitting rage,
And in that moment purest hate engraved
The name of Boudicca on histories page.

In the heart of woman, mother, Queen
Blood had turned to venom in a beat,
Summoning the chieftains of the tribes
She swore an oath that shadowed Rome's defeat.

In Colchester that cold December night
The seventh Galus legion lay to bed,
When from the hills in chariots of steel
Came mayhem, murder, hate and severed head.

Six hundred Romans met their fate that day
And Boudicca was always to the fore,
As she surveyed the ashes of the fort
A voice within her heart had whispered, "More."

She never camped but headed to the south
The firestorm within her burning still,
At Verulamium a thousand died
Then London bled and smouldered at her will

Now ramblers wander in this tranquil place
Unknowing of the passion it has seen,
When bitter vengeance roused a tribe to war
A mother's heart that made a worrier Queen.

Starlight

At dusk the sunset artist paints the sky
In gold and Amber pigment tongues of flame,
Then as the pastel evening yields to night
The blood red crescent moon ascends again.

Suspended in the blackened velvet sky
Countless distant worlds begin to shine,
Each one pulsating energy as light
Each a heartbeat echoing through time.

How can we comprehend this mystery
Our minds too immature to understand,
How when these twinkles started on their way
No human soul had ever trod the land.

And yet the greatest mystery of all
And one the finest minds cannot explain,
If in one second we could reach a star
Ten billion years of journey would remain.

Branigan's Lass

Young Branigan's lass
Had a heart for the chasing,
Laughing her way through
The men of the town.
A glance from her eyes
Sent every pulse racing,
She kept standing them up
And then knocking them down.

A beautiful temptress
A siren among them,
Though seeing the danger
They couldn't resist.
But she was a lass
With insatiable hunger,
So the wealthiest men
Were the top of her list.

Through turbulent nights
Her suitors were dreaming,
Of moments of conquest
When she would succumb.
For not one of them yet
Had tasted the sweetness,
Of her in compliance
As the race had been won.

Nobody counted the hearts
That were broken,
No measure was taken
Of those she deceived.
Now back in her stable
The lady is sleeping,
The bookmakers smile
The punters are grieved.

This Near

She never wanders far beyond my mind
But lingers like a fond remembered dream,
To flash her dear brown eyes for my delight
As sunlight glinting from a rippled stream.

Our shadows merge, cast by the lunar glow
That lights our river walk when evening calls,
And while these blessed hours melt to night
Her fragrance like the scented blossom falls.

And so at times in wanderings you'll find
Me musing on some hills above the sea,
For in such peaceful solitude I know
I hear her spirit speak her love for me.

This Lover's Day

As wisps of clouds desert the skies
A trillion stars caress your eyes,
While all around the echoed sighs
Of hearts immune to lullabies.
Lay wakeful, musing words to say
On this romantic lover's day.

Breezes whisper, rivers glide
As on they wander starry eyed,
The vulgar world is cast aside
Each to the others heart is tied.
And as they dream the night away
They'll live again this lovers' day.

This is the ebb before the flow
As passion's embers warm and glow,
All hearts believe but seldom know
That nature calls for love to grow.
By gilded flecks of dawn we pay
Our homage to this lovers' day.

Where Are They Now?

Where are they now the brave men
The strong men that built the world,
The gruff and seldom shave men
When industry was first unfurled.
What happened to the real men
The steel men who toiled hard,
The boiler men and riveters
Who built the liners in the yard.

Where did they go those fine men
The mine men from underground,
Those stoic never whine men
Who tunnelled where the coal was found.
Did you know the navvy men
Who laboured long for little pay,
To etch the lines across the map
For rails we travel on today.

They have all gone those old men
And cold men to early graves,
Those cheaply bought and sold men
Who lived as little more than slaves.
Now who is left to mourn them
Adorn them in memory,
Those heroes from the old days
Who fired the world with industry.

Le Café Marbella

A Parisian evening
Avec vin ordinaire
Le Café Marbella
Still one empty chair.
Sirens are wailing
Down by the Seine,
As lights on the tower
Make pearls of the rain.

The city of artists
Starts living again,
As laughter dispels
The accordion strain.
They're serving romance
In the riverside bars,
Or dancing on the tables
To Spanish guitars.

It's a year to the hour
We both made a vow,
My heart is distraught
For where are you now.
The candlelight flicker
Danced in your hair,
A Parisian evening
Avec vin ordinaire,

Stills from the Dream

I'm cradled in dreams
In a passionate slumber,
She covers my body
And eases my mind.
Just before sunrise
She kisses me softly,
Leaves me with smiles
Of the sensual kind.

Whenever I falter
She flies to be with me,
Lays her love upon me
As soft as the rain.
She reaches out to me
And turns me to face her,
A smile from those eyes
And I'm living again.

I see her cavorting
In mists over water,
Her laughter rings out
In songs of the breeze.
I feel my heart skip a beat
When she is beside me,
I'll hold het forever
Then beg a reprise.

So Melts Another Day

He sits back in the chair and gently sighs
Shuts the book, rubs fingers on his eyes,
It seems they are less tender than before
Though deep inside the scar is just as sore.
So melts another day, and one day more.

She's hastily untidy round his mind
Spilling memories of things she left behind,
Dropping pictures everywhere as if unsure
Of which to leave in fragments on the floor.
So melts another face, and one face more.

All the while times lazy hands advance
It's healing ways distorted in the dance,
Of silhouettes and shadows from before
That wheel and fade too sinful to endure.
So melts another life, and one life more.

Would You?

Would you stand before God
With your sword unsheathed
And spit in the eye of the storm.
Would you fight to the death
For the things you believed
Forgetting your body was torn.
Would you fly to the stars
Riding Arian's spear,
Pushing the boundaries
Of natural fear.
Risking damnation
For dreams you hold dear.
Would you?

Would you ride into hell
On the Sleipnir steed
And call for the devil to dance.
Would you stand all alone
Gainst the wrath of the world
Certain they hadn't a chance.
Would you stand up and shout
For how it should be,
That all of the world
Could be fed and be free.
Cursing our leaders
Damn hypocrisy.
Would you?

Softly with the Night

She does not come
At dawn's appointed time,
When skies are pale
And stars begin to fade.
When drops of dew
Wake every sleeping flower,
And songbirds tribute
To the day is made.

She does not come
When noon in all its glory,
Is sometimes dazzled
By the ardent light.
And drowsy mayflies
Settle on the water,
To cool their wings
From vacillating flight.

But once the weary
Day embraces slumber,
The world is bathed
In blue seductive light.
She'll gently fold her
Eager wings around me,
Oh how my love
Comes softly with the night.

Dream

I had a dream, where eagles black as night
Were flying high across some bleak terrain,
And each in turn would fly toward the sun
Till steeped in flame they fall to earth again.

Each time a feathered ember touched the sand
It changed at once into a crystal spring,
With veins of water spreading everywhere
That changed the desert into fertile land.

I watched a mix of trees and flowers form
Along the verge of golden fields of grain,
Where people dressed in clothes from other worlds
Bore witness as an age of peace was born.

Wild Birds

Fat balls, the guy had said to me
I never took it personally,
I'd asked for something sugar free.
To feed the wild birds.

They only cost a pound for five
To keep our feathered friends alive,
Snow will fall but they survive.
Our stoic wild birds.

They come in netted sacks of red
Have a smell of something dead,
Food I'd rather not be fed.
Strictly for the birds.

And so I hang them on the tree
A winter gift to you from me,
Each day I love your symphony.
Sweet wild birds.

The Whisperers

Suddenly I'm running
as the path got steeper,
pushed along by gravity
I find I can't oppose.
My hands and face are being torn
by nettle, thorn and creeper,
and darkness hangs upon me
like a suit of cold wet clothes.

Then I'm thrown into a clearing
where no living thing would venture,
all around me flesh is rotting
and I'm sickened by the smell.
Then somewhere in the distance
comes the sound of rolling thunder,
while nearby voices whisper
saying what, I cannot tell.

Now I'm lying in this putrid place
in terror that consumes me,
my heart is like a hammer
on an anvil deep inside.
The thunders rolling nearer
with its flashes of fork lightning,
and the voices are still whispering
saying what, I can't decide.

Now the ground begins to tremble
with a roar to match the thunder,
and the lightning strikes come faster
as the storm is overhead.
Then I feel that I am soaking
for the rain has started falling,
all at once I wake up sweating
once more conscious in my bed.

Wave

Kiss your lips to see you smile
Stroke your hair it's been a while,
Slip my arms around your waist
Pull closer for another taste.
Gently swaying cheek to cheek
Finding words I've longed to speak,
Your body holding tight to mine
Two hearts, one heart beat in time.

Heated blood the pulses chase
Our eager hands unfolding lace,
Fashioned vestures fresh from store
Lay strewn, abandoned on the floor.
All secrets shed as we begin
Our lustful tumble into sin,
We ride that wave that washes deep
Then hold and kiss, and smile, and sleep.

Call to Me

Call to me when troubles of the world
Black as clouds of thunder gather round,
Or gazing up at heaven's host of stars
That which blessed our love cannot be found.

Call to me when daemons of the night
Inveigle fear into your silver dreams,
To whisper doubt in poison- tainted lies
How love has far less beauty than it seems.

Call to me when sorrows fall as rain
Each drop a haunting shadow on your heart,
That wash the rainbow colours from your eyes
Exchanging shades of grey as they depart.

Call to me on precious summer days
When life's a joyful dance and skies are blue,
Although it's just a whisper I will hear
And swim an ocean wide to be with you.

Night Feed

The city's heart beats through the night
The arteries still oozing blood,
That trickles through the urban streets
To meet the dawn and be a flood.

The hangers from the twilight clubs
Dance homeward in the dizzy street,
And sluggish dregs on subway trains
Rub bleary eyes and trampled feet.

The mewing of romancing toms
Gives voice to jealous backyard dogs,
While in a garret, bleary eyed
A bedsit hack is feeding blogs.

The night watch on the juggernauts
Are owl- eyed and diesel fumed,
As thousands dream their way towards
Another day to be consumed.

The Saturday Kid

I was the Saturday kid
Who lived for the movies,
That magic arena
Where fantasies play.
I rode on the prairie
And dived in the ocean,
Then stayed in a rapture
The rest of the day.

I swung through the trees
When I heard Tarzan calling,
For those ivory hunters
Were landing their plane.
But with moments to spare
All the elephants joined us,
And the baddies slunk off
Empty handed again.

I was out on the prairie
With the posse behind me,
Those outlaws were running
From robbing the mail.
I rode up behind them
And fired my pistol,
To a man they surrendered
Then I locked them in jail.

And as the house lights cane on
We all rushed for the exit,
Still riding my stallion
I was out on my own.
I flew with the hawk man
And sailed after pirates,
A kid went to the movies
But a hero went home.

The Carousel

Life is a ride
On a carousel,
Changing seats
To the barker's yell.
How long you'll ride
You can never tell,
As years go spinning
Round.

Take your place
Hear the organ play,
You enjoy the ride
Laughing all the way.
Then the barker says
That you have to pay,
As years go spinning
Round.

Turn to be a kid at play
Turn to see the teenage way,
Turn to work and family
Turn to someone else to be.
What to change to ease the pain
If you could take the ride again.
As years go spinning
Round.

Soon Spring

When first the tender buds appear
And winter's grey is in decline,
The songbirds sing together songs
And bees return to columbine.

Along the kitchen garden wall
Clothed in veils of ivy green,
The final scarlet velvet bloom
Of winter pansies may be seen.

Freshly thawed the sodden earth
Is dried beneath the early sun,
While on the bank are tiny prints
Of paws where baby rabbits run.

The debris twigs from winter storms
Are gathered by the nesting throng,
Like any Mother Nature finds
Means to make her children strong.

Buds and bees and paws and trees
Are signs that winter's race is run,
Now out of time those frosted days
Give way to hope and birth and sun.

Sleep Took me

Sleep took me to a valley with a stream
Born from rocks where wild basil grew
Bartsia, eyebright, marigold and blinks
With clumps of arabis in deepest blue.

It rippled sparkling by a coppice row
Flowered pink with cherry blossom leaves,
That nestled in the folds of patchwork hills
Where purple wild nettles grew in sheaths.

As I followed where the water flowed
The air was never silent on the way,
Songs of lapwing, nightingale and dove
Vied with goldfinch, kingfisher and jay.

The trees were thicker now to form a wood
Where tangled root and coloured fungi grew,
Amid the oak, crab apple, mountain pine
Were silver birch, ash, elm and mystic yew.

The stream had widened now into a pool
Where waterlillies idled in the shade,
Mayflies danced and water boatman rowed
As springtails slept and phantom midges played.

There was a rustic stile by a lane
A rough and ready portal to a place,
Where sleep will carry dreamers in its arms
To rest a while in natures sure embrace.

Clouds

It's a harsh world sometimes
To see dear friends stumble,
You reach out to hold them
But you can't stop their fall.
It's not a matter of weight
Or the distance between you,
But a heart in such anguish
Feels alone after all.

There are times when I wonder
Why the rain started falling,
How the clouds silver lining
Became tarnished with grey.
Then I look to the sunlight
Glowing near the horizon,
No storm lasts forever
And each night yields to day.

If Mine Had Been

If mine had been a painter's eyes
That every shade and tint perceive,
I'd make a portrait of your face
In beauty, love and make believe.

If mine had been a singer's voice
With perfect tone and range of scale,
I'd serenade you every day
With songs of hearts that never fail.

If mine had been a poet's heart,
In words to take your breath away,
I'd pen such verses to our love
And speak them to you every day.

If mine had been a player's hands
Caressing keys to make them ring,
I'd play the soundtrack of your life
In chords sublime to make you sing.

Our Timid Star

Shall we steal away my dear
Our timid star is close at hand,
Its sapphire waters, sparkling clear
Wash shores of saffron tinted sand.

Can we have some time together
On the emerald mountains there,
While all around the crystal peaks
Are shimmering in solar air.

Will we walk that silver path
Into the silent wood we found,
As blossoms from the prism trees
Make rainbow carpets all around.

When the twin suns cease their glow
Triple moons spread purple light,
We'll look back to earth and know
We both are sleeping sound tonight.

Quake

There is a great disquiet in the earth
Nature wakes with anger in her heart,
And raging at the arrogance of man
She forms a frown and tears the world apart.

We strut like gods and envy all we see
Given life yet still we ask for more,
We dare to make a captive of the sun
Then find there is a daemon in the core.

Rivers

They carry all those visions
That you reach for in the morning,
All the shadows of the stories
Only dreamers ever see.
Like a distant fading echo
You were never meant to keep them
They are taken by the river
That meanders to the sea.

They are fragments of a memory
A fraction of a segment,
Just the faintest recollections
From a long forgotten age.
And like prisms in a mirror,
They refract in rainbow colours
They're forever overwriting
Finished stories on your page.

Fog

A fog bank rolled in
Chased by a west wind,
Muffling breakers
Familiar roar.
Dark as a secret
Cold as a warning,
It crept from the ocean
Crawled on the shore.

Silently tumbling
Deep into the city,
Cloaking the street lamps
Familiar glow.
Touching the people
With icy wet fingers,
Featureless shadows
With nowhere to go.

Grey is the pallet
In shades of distortion,
Clinging on buildings
To drape and conceal.
A pale orb is rising
Sun in ascendance,
Strangely diffusing
A dawn that's surreal.

Heart

Is there a place to rest the heart
In times of sorrow and despair,
When souls awake to flaming dawns
With gods and daemons raging there.

When steeped in desperate solitude
The hidden darkness of the mind,
Erupts to overwhelm the whole
And saving grace is disinclined.

So lonely is the human way
How singular the pain inside,
The vaguest path is all that leads
Where faith and hope may still reside.

Once in the Stream

I long to glide once more into that stream
Surrender all this passion to the wave,
Where folding wings encircle all I am
And once again they answer what I crave.

I want to feel those ripples all around
That dance along the pathways to my soul,
Playing notes that never have been found
The music that will make our bodies whole.

It isn't that we need it to survive
Nor without the swimming we'd be lost,
Our love grew from a current to a tide
It freely flows, there never was a cost.

Desio

Desio stands for desire
Deseando que, desiring you,
You have made a spark a fire
Now deseando que, is all I do.

Sólo amor means just loving
Sólo amarte, just loving you,
In my dreams awake and sleeping
Sólo amarte is all I do.

Para siempre means forever
Por siempre, forever you,
For every moment of my life
Por siempre, will be true.

A Bird Unknown

A bird flew up
An arrow from a tree,
A spray of colour
In the gathering grey.
It turned and circled
Calling out its name,
A transient soul
A bird unknown to me.

I stood in awe
Was I just one to see?
This minute's host
This measure of a day.
Were you a gift?
Or only nature's whim
You touched my heart
A bird unknown to me.

Perhaps a captive
Joyful to be free,
Or wayward spirit
From a foreign scene.
I'll never know you
Yet in all my life,
You will remain
A bird unknown to me.

End of an April Day

Much cooler now
As April falls to dusk,
And shadows fall
On days of waking spring.
The silent scented breeze
Has calmed at last
To welcome home
The last birds on the wing.

The silhouetted spires
Formed by the trees,
Reach to the sky
To grasp the fading light.
And all at once
The first array of stars,
Begin to glimmer
Their celestial light.

The flower beds where
Honey bees had played,
Are fallen silent now
And cast in gloom.
Yet now and then
The fingered setting sun,
Will bring to fire
The ember of a bloom.

Echo of a Heartbeat

It was never just the walking
In the shadows touching hands,
Or the pillow talk and loving
Early mornings making plans.
It was more two souls united
Something kismet understands,
And the unrelenting flowing
Of the tine elapsing sands.

It is deeper than caressing
Or the blessing of each day,
More than tears for separation
When the world gets in our way.
It's the passion for each other
When we're lost for words to say,
And the echo of a heartbeat
As the moments steal away.

www.ingramcontent.com/pod-product-compliance
Ingram Content Group UK Ltd.
Pitfield, Milton Keynes, MK11 3LW, UK
UKHW041930190726
13854UKWH00004B/1535